Air is warmed by the sun

Air

Aaron Frisch

A⁺

Smart Apple Media

COPYRIGHT

Published by Smart Apple Media

1980 Lookout Drive, North Mankato, MN 56003

Designed by Rita Marshall

Copyright © 2002 Smart Apple Media. International copyright reserved in all countries. No part of this book may be reproduced in any form without written permission from the publisher.

Printed in the United States of America

Photographs by KAC Productions (Kathy Adams Clark, Larry Ditto), Tom Myers

Library of Congress Cataloging-in-Publication Data

Frisch, Aaron. Air / by Aaron Frisch. p. cm. – (Elements series)

Includes index.

ISBN 1-58340-073-7

1. Air–Juvenile literature. [1. Air.] I. Title. II. Elements series (North Mankato, Minn.)

QC161.2 .F75 2001   533–dc21   00-067974

First Edition 9 8 7 6 5 4 3 2 1

$\mathcal{A}$ir

CONTENTS

What Is Air?

Air is all around us, keeping us alive. We can't see it, smell it, or taste it, but it is as real as land or water. It can blow houses down, carry water around the world, and support huge objects such as jets. Without air, Earth would be nothing but a large, lifeless rock. Air is the mixture of gases that surrounds the earth. There are many different kinds of gases in air, but the main ones are nitrogen and oxygen. Oxygen is especially important, since humans and animals need to breathe

Air is invisible to the naked eye

this gas to stay alive. The air around the earth is called

the atmosphere. It is made up of several layers. The layer clos-

est to the earth is called the troposphere. This is where most of

the air's gases are found. Air gets colder very high in the

atmosphere. The atmosphere ends about 1,000 miles (1,610

km) above the earth, where the air fades into outer space.

Air Particles and Weight

The air is full of invisible particles called aerosols.

Aerosols are kind of like dust. They come from car exhaust,

volcano smoke, and other things. Even a tiny amount of air—

like the air inside a balloon—contains millions of them.

Aerosols are a natural part of the air, but too many of them can

cause **pollution**. The air over big cities that have a lot of cars

The atmosphere above a layer of clouds

Air allows our planet to support life

and factories is often polluted. ⟿ Air also contains tiny drops of water called water vapor. Water vapor is the moisture that enters the air when heat from the sun makes water in lakes and the ocean **evaporate**. If the air gets cool enough, water vapor turns into bigger drops of water and falls to the earth as rain. In even colder air, water vapor turns into ice crystals and falls as snow. ⟿ Air has weight, but it is so light that people usually don't notice it. At **sea level**, the amount of air that fits inside a shoe box weighs about one ounce (13.8 g). The atmosphere is made up of many layers of air. The weight of

each layer presses down on the air below it. This downward

force is called air pressure. There is less air pressure high in the

atmosphere, since there is less air pushing down.

Fog is a cloud of water vapor close to the earth

Wind and Motion

Moving air is called wind. Wind is caused by the sun. As the sun heats the earth, the ground gets heated unevenly. Warm air is lighter than cold air, so it rises. The air over warm ground heats up and rises higher into the atmosphere. Cooler air then rushes in to take its place near the earth's surface, creating wind. Air resists the motion of objects traveling through it. As objects move through air, they rub against aerosols and **molecules** in the air. This slows the

Falling rain washes many aerosols from the air. This is why the air seems fresher after it rains.

objects down. The air slows down wide objects more than nar-

row ones. This is why parachutes fall slowly to the ground, and

why airplanes cut through the air very fast. The faster

Windsurfers catching wind in their sails

an object moves, the more the air tries to slow it down. If an

object moves through the air fast enough, this resistance cre-

ates **friction**. Friction causes heat. When objects from outer

space—such as meteors and space shut-

tles—enter Earth's atmosphere, they are

moving so fast that the resistance makes

them very hot. Space shuttles are built to

Sometimes people's ears "pop" when they ride up an elevator or a steep hill. This is caused by changing air pressure.

withstand this heat, but most meteors and other falling objects

burn up in the atmosphere.

Fire cannot exist without the oxygen in air

Helping the Earth

Air helps us in many ways. Without the oxygen in air, humans and animals could not breathe. Air also allows us to hear by carrying **sound waves**. In places that don't have air—such as outer space—there can be no sound. Ozone, a kind of gas in the air, forms a barrier around the earth called the ozone layer.

A small amount of air at the edge of the atmosphere is always leaking into outer space. But it will take billions of years for all of the earth's air to escape.

The ozone layer blocks certain kinds of rays from the sun that

Air helps protect and warm the earth

can harm people. Air also keeps the earth warm. It allows some of the sun's rays to enter the atmosphere, then traps the heat so it can't escape back into space. This is known as the greenhouse effect. By keeping the planet warm and allowing living things to breathe, air helps to make Earth a cen- ter of life in the universe.

Scientists study air pressure and air temperatures to help predict the weather.

All plants and animals need air to live

Weighing Air

Even though we usually can't feel it, air has weight. You can see this for yourself with a simple experiment.

What You Need

Tape	A ruler
Thread	Two balloons of equal size

What You Do

1. Tie a piece of thread around the middle of the ruler.
2. Lift the ruler by the thread. Slide the thread so that the ruler balances evenly. Then add a piece of tape to keep the thread from sliding.
3. Blow up one balloon. Blow up the other balloon to be about half as big as the first one. Use the tape to attach them to opposite ends of the ruler.
4. Hold up the ruler by the thread and watch what happens. The end of the ruler with the bigger balloon will dip lower. This happens because the bigger balloon has more air in it, making it heavier than the smaller one.

Air gives an inflated balloon weight

Index

Words to Know

evaporate (ee-VAP-uh-rate)—to turn a liquid into a gas form called vapor

friction (FRIK-shun)—the rubbing of two objects against each other

molecules (MOL-uh-kyuls)—tiny, moving particles that make up a substance

pollution (puh-LOO-shun)—a state when the environment contains dirty or harmful substances

sea level (SEE lev-ul)—ground that is level with the surface of the ocean

sound waves (SOWND wayvs)—vibrations that create the sounds we hear

Read More

Baines, John D. *Keeping the Air Clean.* Austin, Tex.: Raintree Steck-Vaughn, 1998.

Miller, Christina G., and Louise A. Berry. *Air Alert: Rescuing the Earth's Atmosphere.* New York: Atheneum Books, 1996.

Yount, Lisa, and Mary M. Rodgers. *Air.* Minneapolis: Lerner Publications, 1995.

Internet Sites

Air Pollution—U.S. Environmental Protection Agency
http://www.epa.gov/oar/

Project Clean Air
http://www.projectcleanair.org/

Clean Air Act
http://www.epa.gov/oar/oaq_caa.html